DEFUSING THE BOMB

A GUIDE TO UNDERSTANDING AND

DEALING WITH A NARCISSIST AND

HEALING FROM NARCISSISTIC ABUSE

CHARLOTTE REED

Thank You for purchasing this book,

I'd like to give you a free gift.

Go to charlottereedit.com

to get your free gift

Table of Contents

INTRODUCTION

Over the decades, narcissism has sparked a lot of interest in the world of psychology and psychoanalytic. It has become a topical and highly controversial issue in the field of science. Even so, many of us have no idea what narcissism is and what it entails.

Narcissism is a modern day epidemic that keeps spreading its reach in the society. Clearly, Narcissists are everywhere around us, which is why it is very crucial for us to understand this epidemic and the people it affects. Like a bomb, every narcissist is waiting to explode in our face.

Most people mistake narcissism for arrogance. But in truth, narcissism goes beyond arrogance. It is a malicious personality disorder that can destroy our relationships and family. For people who have one or more narcissist in their lives (parents, spouse), this book has been written to help them gain more insights into narcissism and what it means to have a narcissistic individual in their lives.

In this book, we will be going through a lot of topics on the subject: Narcissism and Narcissistic Personality Disorder. This book will examine what narcissism really means, the myth behind narcissism and the people who we refer to as narcissists. Furthermore, we will discuss the submissions of learned psychologists and psychoanalysts on

Narcissism. If you are in a relationship with a narcissist or you have been a subject of narcissistic abuse, and you don't even know it, this book will also put you through on how to recognize narcissism and deal with narcissistic abuse.

"Narcissistic Abuse: Understanding Narcissistic Personality Disorder and Healing from Narcissistic Abuse" is a must-read for anybody who has been thirsting for knowledge on narcissism for long. The book is written in a simplified language to help ease smooth understanding. Read on as you unravel the mystery that is Narcissism!

CHAPTER ONE

WHAT DO YOU KNOW ABOUT

NARCISSISM?

The word "Narcissism" has a particular image it brings to the mind when mentioned or heard. This image is usually one of unhealthy self-love, self-centeredness, and an over-bloated sense of importance. This is what you probably think of too when you think of a narcissist; someone with a grandiose sense of self. As apt as this may seem, narcissism is more than this mental image we construct of it. Narcissism is one of the most interesting topics of discussion in Psychology, and this is due to the amount of misunderstanding and misconception that surrounds it.

Narcissism is subjective to different interpretations, depending on individual point of view. To some people, narcissism is considered to be a way of showing oneself a healthy and considerable amount of self-love. While this point of view on narcissism may be right, there comes the point where you have to draw the line between narcissism as a form of self-love and a psychological disorder.

According to Google, Narcissism is an excessive interest in or admiration of oneself and one's physical appearance. From this definition, we deduce that narcissism centers on self-absorption; the act of being consumed in admiration and awe of oneself. This should naturally be a good and desirable trait. However, the definition also makes use of the word "excessive" which tells us that self-absorption or self-love is okay but, it gets out of hand and becomes narcissistic only when it gets to an unacceptable degree.

Apart from this definition of narcissism by Google, Psychology has a more pronounced definition which goes "selfishness, involving a sense of entitlement, a lack of empathy, and a need for admiration, as characterizing a personality type." Looking at this psychological definition of narcissism, it shows that narcissism goes beyond being absorbed in oneself. And, this is where the degree of narcissism comes in. Anyone can be a narcissist; I can be a narcissist, and you can be a narcissist. In fact, every human has tendencies of narcissism although it is more prominent in some than others. So, how is "narcissism" measured before it becomes diagnosed as a clinical disorder?

Narcissism can be a healthy thing; it motivates us to love ourselves and constantly reminds us of our worth, so we don't fall below expectations or let others take us for granted. However, it becomes a disorder when it begins to interfere with the way we think, behave and relate with people around us. What this means is that some degree of narcissism may be a good thing but once it starts to affect the way we reason, interact with and perceive others, it is no longer just "self-love" but an impairment of our personality. Narcissism becomes "Narcissistic Personality Disorder" when your ability to function independently and engage with others rationally and naturally becomes nonexistent. Usually, people suffering from NPD have fragile and vulnerable self-esteem which they try to hide behind a facade of extreme confidence, excessive attention-seeking and little or no empathy for others. To keep up with the facade, they have an insatiable need for validation and approval from others. When it seems like they aren't getting enough validation and admiration as they would like, it results in a mental meltdown and feelings of inadequacy.

Now, you have a more informed idea on what "Narcissism" is and what it should mean to you aside everybody's general perception of this topical psychology phenomenon. In the next chapter, we will be taking an in-depth look at the psychological perception of narcissism, the roots and the origin of the word "Narcissism" itself!

THE ROOTS OF NARCISSISM

The history of the word 'narcissism' can be traced back to the Greek mythology about the dashing young hunter 'Narcissus' who was widely renowned for his exceptional beauty. One day, while Narcissus was on a hunt in the woods, he stops by a still, silver pond for a cool drink of water. As he kneels by the pond for a drink, he catches a reflection of himself and falls in love with his reflection. Narcissus said to the reflection "I love you." Narcissus was so in love with the image that he became unable to pull his attention away and becomes absorbed in the image. He lost the zeal to eat, and drink; all he wanted to do was staring at his reflection in the pool all day, all night. Eventually, absorbed and consumed by own reflection in the pool, Narcissus withers away and dies. After his death, Narcissus transforms into the beautiful flower that now shares his name.

From the myth of Narcissus, we can tell that he was someone who was enamored and wholly absorbed in himself; giving no regard to any other thing. The story of Narcissus doesn't end here however; it extends to a story about Narcissus and a maiden called "Echo." The story of Narcissus and Echo will be continued in a chapter which focuses on narcissism, narcissistic abuse and how it affects relationships.

The British physician, Havelock Ellis was the first person to identify narcissism as a mental disorder in 1898. He characterizes narcissism as a pathological self-absorption, accompanied by an inflated self-image. Narcissism is a disorder that is common more in men than women, and a large percent of NPD originates from childhood.

According to the famous psychoanalyst, Sigmund Freud, narcissism is a part of child development but should be considered a disorder if the traits persist in children after puberty. As kids, children are understandably and naturally selfish. It is a normal part of biological development which makes them concerned about getting their needs met, and being unable to understand other people' needs or desires. As they develop into teenagers, they retain this trait of self-centeredness because they are in a phase where they struggle for independence. Although children need to develop a healthy level of self-esteem as they grow up, this self-centeredness is something that should naturally decline. A healthy self-esteem is essential for them to be able to protect and care for themselves, while also retaining care for others. This will enable them to formulate lasting social relationships with family, friends and others in the society. Self-esteem isn't the same as self-centeredness, however. A person with a healthy self-esteem doesn't put themselves first at the detriment of others. But, a narcissistic person will because they are unable to get rid of their self-centeredness which developed with them as a part of childhood. Narcissists generally try to excuse or defend their disorder by characterizing it as having a high self-esteem. In a subsequent chapter, we will be discussing the clinical theories of narcissism developed by psychoanalysts such as Heinz Kohut and Otto Kernberg explains more on the root of narcissism. However, before we do that, let's take a look at the early submissions on narcissism by philosophers and thinkers.

Initially, narcissism was referred to as hubris by early philosophers. Hubris was regarded as a state of extreme arrogance and pride which causes people to be out of touch with reality. It then developed into recognition as a state of excessive self-admiration, after which it became an area of interest in the field of psychology. The earliest description of narcissism was by the Austrian psychoanalyst Otto Rank. He described narcissism as being connected to vanity and self-admiration. However, more famous was the submission of Sigmund Freud in a paper published in 1914 and titled, On Narcissism: An Introduction.

Freud had a number of ideas on how narcissism manifests in a person. According to him, it was connected to a person's libido (the energy behind human survival instinct) and whether it is directed outward toward others or inward toward oneself. Freud proposed that infants directed all of their libido inward which was understandable since they are still in the early stage of development, and he called this primary narcissism. He also said that there was a designated amount of libido which if directed outward toward others would diminish the amount available for oneself. What this means is that if you direct your entire libido outward, you're giving all your love away to people around you and probably leaving none available for yourself. Freud noted that this makes people experience a decline in primary narcissism. And, for the libido to be replenished, a person will also have to receive a healthy amount of love in return. This is what would help maintain a sense of satisfaction in everyone. In other words, you have to get back all the love you give out.

Freud's theory on narcissism also added that a person's sense of self develops right from when he is a child, interacting with the outside world and learning social and cultural norms. From this, it develops into an image of oneself that we strive to reach. He recognized that the love of oneself could be transmitted to another person or object. Freud suggests that this helps people experience a diminishment of primary narcissism which leaves them unable to nurture, defend and protect themselves. In order for them to be able to do this, they also had to receive love and affection in return for a balance to be maintained. Narcissism however became recognized as a mental disorder because of the studies of Kornberg and Kohut which sparked more interest in the topic.

However, one thing that we must all recognize and accept is that narcissism isn't about superiority. Rather, it is more about a feeling of vulnerability which narcissists try so hard to hide behind their mask of unfazed confidence and faux self-esteem. The root of narcissism lies at the unwillingness of a narcissist to show even the tiniest sign of vulnerability with anybody because they don't want to be seen as weak or taken advantage of. Narcissists lack trust for others, even those they are close with and as a result of this; they avoid putting themselves in a situation where they are vulnerable with others. The central idea of narcissism is about a resistance to vulnerability rather than superiority as most people think. When the cloaks of grandiosity and superiority are taken off a narcissist, you will find only a person constantly in a state of hyper-vigilance and anxiety.

To truly understand a narcissist, you must see into their mind and know for yourself how it works. How does a narcissist think? Do they really feel like they are superior to others or is it all a show; a facade behind which they hide the feeling of weakness? Once we know and understand how the mind of a narcissist works, it becomes easier to live with and stay in a relationship with one.

HOW DOES A NARCISSIST'S MIND WORK?

Often, when you think of a narcissist, you think of a person who is incredibly arrogant and self-assured; a person who is obsessed with the way he looks and likes to be the center of attraction. Science and psychology also describe narcissists as people who possess certain distinguishing traits such as a sense of entitlement and need excessive admiration. These positions are all quite correct. But, have you ever wondered how a narcissist really thinks of himself? How does a narcissist see himself?

A narcissist sees himself as being special and better than others. He thinks that the world should revolve around him and everybody should always have a special word of admiration for him. Narcissists view themselves as being preferentially different when compared to other people. They want everything to be about them and as such, struggle desperately for even the littlest of attention and admiration from others. Take for instance; a 3-year old might constantly seek for attention because he/she is at a developmental stage where he should; that is understandably appropriate. However, what do you think of a 30-40-year-old who wants the same level of attention as a 3-year old? It says a lot. Here are just a few of the thoughts that roam about in the mind of a narcissist:

- I love myself, and everybody else does too: A narcissist thinks everybody is obligated to love him as he loves himself. In fact, he cannot and will not entertain the thought and possibility of you not loving him as he expects. A little sign that not everybody feels about him the way he wishes and a narcissist develops a feeling of inadequacy and incompleteness.

- I don't owe anybody an apology: Narcissists expect you to understand, accept and tolerate them with all their faults, no matter what. They feel like they do not need to apologize when they do something wrong. A narcissist thinks, "Yeah, I did something wrong but you should understand and accept me for who I am. I don't need to apologize to you."

- I am better than everybody else: A narcissist believes he has few equals in the world. He is the best in everything; the most beautiful, the most intelligent, the smartest and what have you. Nobody a narcissist meets is ever better than them.

- I could never be equal with you, or anybody else: A narcissist will constantly rub it in your face and remind you of their achievements, and how you will never measure up. Oh, I do well in school better than you. I am smarter. I am everything you could never be and you need to always remember that.

- I have the right to criticize others but nobody else can criticize me: Don't ever try to criticize a narcissist or they will come at you with rage. A narcissist thinks and believes that they reserve the sole right to criticism and nobody else has the right to criticize them. If you do, they will never forgive you.

- I am not interested in what you have to say, but you must be interested in my achievements and what I have to say: A narcissist cares only about himself. He will constantly remind you of all his numerous achievements, and bother you with his tales of valor. You, on the other hand, must not try to bore him with your stories and achievement because he finds them needless and inconsequential. He is simply not interested.

These are just some of the many thoughts you will find in the head of a narcissist. All of these boil down to the narcissist thinking he has more value than others. A narcissist will always overvalue himself and devalue you; that's how his mind works.

The mind of a narcissist is also preoccupied with fantasies of power, success, beauty, brilliance and love. Now, this isn't such a bad thing except for the part that says "preoccupied." This can be quite hurtful to people around him because he will be consumed only with thoughts of himself, and nobody else would matter. The only thing that would make you matter to a narcissist is if he thinks or believes that you hold the power to help him achieve the perfection he so desperately seeks. But, if you ever show signs of wanting to be far ahead of him, a narcissist will do everything in his power to take you down and ensure you never achieve more than him.

Another thing about narcissists is that they require constant and excessive admiration from their partners or people around them generally. The narcissist can be described as an empty emotional vessel which needs to be constantly refueled with admiration, compliments, and praises. For instance, a narcissistic boyfriend needs you to always tell him that he's beautiful, strong and more than a lady can wish for. However, don't expect this to be reciprocal. The fact that he wants you to tell him this all the time doesn't mean he's going to return you the favor of showering you with compliments or praises too. Narcissism is all about "take," not "give and take."

One question that comes to mind is, why does a narcissist think like this? Why does his mind work like this? The answer to this is pretty simple. A narcissist doesn't trust you and doesn't want you to see him as weak or vulnerable; therefore he constantly puts you down and devalues you to project himself as strong, confident and self-assured. Think about it: we can't all feel great or confident about ourselves all the time even though narcissists fervently try to. In the mind of a narcissist, "I can't show any sign of weakness. If I do, people will want to take advantage of me. I must show them that I'm better and superior to them."

This shows that the narcissist fears being vulnerable before others. Therefore, he keeps up his facade and stomps on any occasional feeling of weakness or vulnerability by projecting himself to be more powerful and stronger than he actually feels.

In a nutshell, a narcissist thinks only about himself. The thoughts of a narcissist are centered solely on himself, his beauty, success and achievements. Don't you ever think you will find yourself in a narcissist's thoughts! He simply doesn't have the space to share.

THE DISTINCTIVE DIFFERENCE BETWEEN NARCISSISM AND NARCISSISTIC PERSONALITY DISORDER

A lot of us are confused about the differences between narcissism and narcissistic personality disorder. Are there really any differences, or are they both the same? If a person is narcissistic, does it mean he automatically has narcissistic personality disorder? These are some of the questions we have in mind.

Narcissism and Narcissistic personality disorder are two sides of a coin yet; they aren't the same. There are some distinct differences that set a narcissistic person apart from a person who has narcissistic personality disorder.

What is Narcissistic Personality Disorder? Narcissistic personality disorder, according to the Mayo Clinic, is a mental disorder in which people have an inflated sense of their own importance and a deep need for admiration. Narcissistic Personality Disorder is regarded as a maladaptive pattern of thoughts and behaviors that occur in thinking, emotion, impulse control and interaction with others. People with narcissistic personality disorder are usually of the thought they are superior to others, and they lack empathy for others' feelings. However, beneath their mask of ultra-confidence hides a fragile self-esteem, vulnerable to the slightest of criticisms.

This mask they put on makes it difficult to understand who they really are. For instance, a typical narcissist comes off as arrogant, cocky and standoffish. However, behind this mask of arrogance they put on, what you will really find is a person with a sense of inferiority and a non-existent self-esteem. This explains why they break down fast in the face of criticism. People like this alienate themselves from family, friends and the society, leading to a feeling of isolation and depression. Narcissistic personality disordered persons are caught between a feeling of superiority and misery.

The difference between narcissism and NPD lies in how it affects the mental health or state of the subject. There is what is known as healthy narcissism which is actually considered good and normal in every person's life. However, it becomes a full-blown mental disorder when the subject starts exhibiting certain traits and symptoms that are considered unhealthy for their mental state and that of others.

A person can be narcissistic without suffering from a mental disorder. A narcissistic person is an obnoxious person who feels he is superior to others and doesn't consider that as being wrong. He feels little or no empathy with the feelings, plight, conditions or situations of people around. He has a deep sense of entitlement and thinks he has the sole right to the best of everything while typically looking down on people who admire him. A narcissist sees nothing wrong in throwing others on the bus if it would benefit him; he exploits others to his advantage and has no difficulty doing it. One important thing to know is that this kind of person isn't self-aware or insightful; therefore; he feels no shame or remorse for any of his actions.

The distinctive difference between a narcissist and a narcissistic personality disordered person is that a narcissist isn't mentally ill doesn't have a personality disorder and is primarily concerned with power, money and honor. Narcissists almost always find their ways to the top or wherever they choose because of their lack of empathy, and the abundance of faux self-esteem.

Going back to the story of Narcissus, we could characterize him as a narcissistic personality disordered person rather than a person with normal narcissism. Think about it: if Narcissus had simply looked at himself in the pool for some minutes and said something like "Dude, you're so beautiful. Wow, no one looks better!" that would have been okay. That would have been normal narcissism. It's normal and okay to recognize something about oneself and brag about it; it points to a healthy self-esteem. However, Narcissus allowed his admiration of himself consume him to the point that nothing else mattered again; to the detriment of his health which eventually led to his death. That is narcissistic personality disorder in its most obvious form. Let's take a look at some of the aspects that distinguish Normal Narcissism from Narcissistic Personality Disorder;

Self-esteem

A person with NPD has an insufficient level of self-esteem. While it may seem like their self-esteem is at its peak to others, it is usually just an act to cover up for the desperately scared little person inside of them. This feeling of inferiority and low self-worth drives their need for constant and excessive admiration, reassurance and praises from others. On the other hand, a person with normal narcissism has a sufficient level of positive and healthy self-esteem, even if they throw it in others' face all the time.

Relationship

People with NPD are severely insecure; therefore they surround themselves with people to sing their praises and stroke their egos. They always want to make sure that they are the most powerful, the smartest, the most beautiful and the most accomplished among any group of persons they find themselves. Once they see a person who looks or appears better, the feeling of extreme insecurity takes over and they become threatened. They choose their relationships with others based on how useful they consider the person. If a person no longer fits their agenda, they drop whatever relationship they have with the person. A normal narcissist, on the other hand, isn't all that bad. He doesn't need others to feel adequate, superior or secure in himself. A person with Normal Narcissism isn't threatened by the achievements of others; he only wants to be better.

Empathy

Not all narcissists lack the capacity for empathy. Most times, it is only those with the personality disorder who are unable to empathize with the feelings or plights of others. A person with NPD will empathize or sympathize with others only if it benefits them and it is all an act. They do not care about others, only themselves. In comparison, an ordinary narcissist has the ability to empathize; they, however, may choose to or not.

Criticism

Narcissistic personality disordered persons do not appreciate or entertain criticism from others. They are overly sensitive and reactive to any form of criticism or slight from others. It shouldn't be surprising to find them blame others for their actions rather than take responsibility. They never take the responsibility for awful decision making or offensive behaviors.

True narcissists (NPD) are different in the sense that they have an unhealthy preoccupation with themselves, and their need for admiration never gets satiated. They are always scared and anxious that there's someone out there more capable, beautiful, successful and competent than them. This is where their disorder lies.

SYMPTOMS OF NARCISSISM AND
NARCISSISTIC PERSONALITY DISORDER

Narcissism isn't easy to spot in a person, especially because of the way the subjects manage to project their vulnerability as confidence. You may be dating a narcissist and you won't even know it. Our parents, our best friend or even our boss at work may all be narcissists but we will never be able to know this unless we know what the symptoms of narcissism and narcissistic personality disorder are.

If you're in a relationship with someone who thinks they are perfect and without fault and never misses the chance to rub it in; chances are you're dating a narcissist. If your parent is the type who expects you to make an 'A' in school all the time without considering your feelings; there is every possibility that they are narcissistic. If your boss at work has an extra puff in his shoulder and is always imposing his authority on his employees; he is also probably a narcissist. If your best friend needs you to make them feel good about themselves every time and gets angry at you when you don't; you might be friends with a narcissist. However, you will never be able to truly identify a narcissist or someone suffering from NPD unless you know the symptoms which they exhibit. Here are symptoms to watch out for to detect narcissism in a person:

- Grandiose sense of self-importance: Grandiosity is central to narcissism and narcissistic personality disorder. This goes above arrogance, pride, or vanity; it is an absurd sense of superiority which narcissists feel they have over others. Narcissists believe they are special and unique and as such, they can only be understood by people of equal 'special' status. Even more, they believe that they deserve more than the average or ordinary; they are made to have the best of everything in life. Interestingly, narcissists want you to praise and admire them even when they have done nothing to earn your admiration. They exaggerate their achievements and importance to feel good about themselves and make you believe they are far better than you. A narcissist never talks about "us," rather all you will hear from him are stories of his success, his contributions, his greatness and how lucky people around him are to have him in their lives. He doesn't think he is lucky to have anyone though; he deserves it all.

- Excessive need for admiration: Does your partner in a relationship want you to tell them how beautiful or great they are in bed all the time? That's another symptom of narcissism.

Narcissists have an insatiable need for constant and excessive admiration from others. Without a steady stream of admirations and praises from people, the narcissist's feeling of superiority becomes misery. A narcissist needs constant admiration to keep his sense of superiority inflated. Note that they do not need occasional compliments; the type we are all comfortable getting from people once in a while. Instead, this is like food for them and so, they surround themselves with praise singers who can cater to their need for applause and recognition. However, this isn't transactional. Compliment a narcissist all the time and he still may not recognize or compliment you in return. Rather, he believes he deserves all the compliments he gets from you and you deserve nothing from him. After all, he is better and more achieved than you. If you ever stop the train of praises, you will be considered and treated as a betrayal.

- Delusions of fantasy: To live up to their grandiose view of themselves which reality doesn't support, narcissists resort to a fantasy island that is fueled by deception, distortion and delusions. Narcissists fantasize about unlimited success, brilliance, power, beauty and the perfect love which give them that feeling of specialness and uniqueness they crave desperately for, and make them feel like they are in control. The delusions and fantasies are ways of protecting themselves from the feelings of inner emptiness and deep shame which they hide behind a mask. The feelings of delusions help to wave away opinions and facts that contradict their view of themselves. Once they meet or encounter anything that threatens to burst their bubble of fantasy, such a thing is met with great resistance and defensiveness and sometimes rage. Therefore, people around narcissists have to learn to be cautious around denying them their distorted view of reality.

- A sense of entitlement: Based on their view of themselves as special and unique, narcissists believe they are entitled to favorable treatment from others. They believe that whatever they want, they should get. Narcissists expect people around them to automatically comply with their every need and wish; this is what gives you value in their eyes. You're useless to them if you can't help them achieve the perfection they crave.

- Perfectionism: Narcissists have the unexplainable need to be perfect, and have everything around perfect. This is as a result of their sense of entitlement which makes them feel like they deserve the best of everything. A narcissist wants to be perfect, wants you to be perfect, wants everything to go their way always, and want life to pan out exactly as they envision it.

Perfectionism is impossible and when the narcissist realizes this, it results in a feeling of misery and dissatisfaction.

- Lack of empathy: One thing about narcissists is that they have little capacity to empathize or sympathize with others. A narcissist is selfish, self-motivated, and is generally unable to understand anybody else's feeling. He expects you to think, reason and, feel exactly as he does and would never give a thought to your own feeling. This trait makes it impossible for them to apologize, feel remorse or guilt. The lack of empathy by the narcissist is caused by their inability to understand feelings. A narcissist cannot understand body language or gestures; therefore he misreads them most times; he is never able to perceive what another person is feeling or thinking accurately. He also doesn't understand the nature of feelings. Narcissists believe that their feelings are caused by external factors such as you rather than their own thoughts, interpretations and biochemistry makeup. What this means that when a narcissist feels bad or negative, you will always be blamed because they are unable to understand how feelings come about. This lack of empathy makes it impossible for a narcissist to experience true emotional connection with anybody.

- Exploitation of others: Narcissists lack the ability to put themselves in the shoes of others. Therefore, they exploit others to their own advantage. This lack of empathy makes them view people in their lives as objects which are there just to satisfy their every need. As a result of this, they don't give taking advantage of others to achieve their own ends a second thought before they do it. Sometimes, narcissists do this in the form of manipulation but most times, they are simply oblivious to what they are doing; they have no idea they are doing anything wrong. Even if you point it out to them, they still won't get it. The only thing narcissists understand is their own needs.

- Obsession with control: The realization that life can never be as perfect as they want it results in the narcissist becoming obsessed with controlling and shaping the events in their life as they want. They become obsessed with being in control, and their sense of entitlement further strengthens their belief that they should be in control of everything always. A typical narcissist has a plot in his head about what every character he interacts with should say and do to him. Once you don't behave like they expect you to, it results in a feeling of anxiety and anger. That feeling of anxiety emerges as a result of their inability to control you, and have you act according to their script. In a narcissist' mind, you are just a character in their story and not an actual person capable of having your own thoughts and feelings.

- Inability to take responsibility: The narcissist wants to be in control but he never wants to be responsible for the consequences of his actions and decisions; unless it goes exactly as he planned. When things don't go according to their plan, and they feel the slightest criticism or realize that they are less than perfect; a narcissist finds somebody else to put all the blame and responsibility on and that's usually you. It is never the fault of a narcissist but the fault of somebody else. The narcissist might blame his mother, the law, a particular rule but often, the person he shifts the blame to most is the most emotionally present, most loyal, most attached and most loving person in his life-you. To keep up with the charade of perfection, narcissists always find another person to take responsibility for their inadequacies.

- Lack of boundaries: Narcissists simply don't know when to draw the line; they don't see where they end and someone else begins. In truth, narcissists are more like 2-year-olds. They are of the belief that everything belongs to them, everyone thinks and feels exactly as they do, and everybody wants the same thing they do. So, it always comes as a shock when they get no for an answer; they will never accept no. Rather than respect your decision and recognize the boundary, a narcissist will go to any length to get whatever they want from you; persistence, demanding, insistence, cajoling, pouting, rejecting or manipulation. Their lack of empathy and inability to understand feelings make it difficult for them to understand why anyone would tell them no or deny them something. Why would you? You're supposed to respond to their every need and take care of every wish and whims they have. If you ever tell him no, he'll do anything to get you to change your answer to a yes.

- Emotional reasoning: Have you ever tried to get the narcissist in your life to understand the effects of his actions on you through logical reasoning? You must have realized that was a waste of time and a mistake. A narcissist has no capacity for emotional or logical reasoning; therefore he will never understand the effects of his actions on you. Narcissists are only aware of their own thoughts and feelings. So, they make decisions and take actions based solely on how they feel about something. A narcissist wants to buy that red designer dress based entirely on how good she would look in it, not whether it will make a dent in the family's budget. If a narcissist becomes bored or unhappy in a relationship, they don't try to make it work; they simply end it and move on to a new relationship. They simply can't understand anything outside their own thoughts and feelings.

Once you identify these signs and traits in a person, it goes beyond doubt that they are narcissistic. Then, it becomes imperative for you to try to understand them or simply move on with your life, depending on your choice. However, it is better most times to not try to understand and cope with a narcissist as they will only tire you out and use you until they have no need for you again. You should only learn to understand and cope with a narcissist if they are a close family member such as your parent.

CHAPTER TWO

WHAT DOES SCIENCE SAY ABOUT

NARCISSISM?

The subject of narcissism is one that draws so many interest and intrigue. For centuries, many people have wondered what narcissism is about. But now, the interest in narcissism has heightened even more, and scientists now refer to this personality disorder as a modern epidemic.

Narcissism was first made popular by the work of the psychoanalyst, Sigmund Freud, like we discussed. The work of Freud was the origin of the development of different theories on narcissism. As interesting as the subject of narcissism is, it begs the question "What does science say about narcissism?"

Scientists believe that narcissism lies between continuums of healthy to pathological. There is what is referred to as healthy narcissism; this is regarded as a normal part of human functioning. Healthy narcissism represents positive self-love, self-esteem, and confidence. It stems from real achievements, having the ability to overcome difficulties and setbacks and more importantly, the support generated from social ties.

However, narcissism becomes pathological when the individual becomes preoccupied with thoughts and fantasies of the self, requiring excessive admiration from others while being insensitive to the feelings of people around. If a narcissist is unable to receive the admiration and attention he craves, it could result in major depressive disorder and substance abuse.

Science posits that narcissism becomes narcissistic personality disorder only when the symptoms and traits become pronounced in an individual to the extent of causing personality impairment. According to statistics, men and younger people are the ones most affected by the disorder. Also, the exact causes of narcissism have yet to be pinpointed, but childhood abuse and neglect are considered to be major possible factors in the development of narcissism. In clinical settings, about 2% to 16% of individuals are said to suffer from Narcissistic personality disorder (NPD) while only 1% of the general population is said to be affected by the disorder. Some scientists are of the opinion that NPD is quite uncommon in people; however, a study has shown that estimates vary largely based on narcissistic traits assessment methods and the sample sizes used for conducting research.

Contrary to what many people think about narcissism- as a disorder based off an inflated self-esteem, and over-bloated sense of importance, narcissism is actually a disorder of self-esteem. Narcissists are usually the ones with the most insecurity in a group of people, but somehow, they have learned to project themselves as anything but that. A narcissist will look like the most confident person in the room to you, but he's actually just an empty soul hoping you don't find him out. There are four things that are central to true narcissism or Narcissistic Personality Disorder, and these are:

- Grandiosity
- Lack of empathy
- Sense of entitlement
- Excessive need for admiration

These are considered to be the core of the disorder, and they all go back to one thing which is fragile self-esteem. The fragility of the self-esteem of a narcissist is what makes him put on a show of grandiosity and superiority.

Like we said, social scientists now label narcissism as a modern epidemic, and societal change in industrial and post-industrial times are believed to be the cause. Over the last few decades, society has witnessed a shift from the collective commitment to individualism and focus on the self. What this means is that we had evolved from a time when everything used to be about the collective and the society as a whole to a time where everyone now champions his cause. This has resulted in the rise of the narcissism rate among individuals.

Individualism has witnessed a rise, and this has resulted in a shift from what is best for the family or society to what is best for me.

Technology and social media are also considered as major factors in the rise of individualism and inevitably, narcissism. Take for instance: the growth of largely popular social media networks such as Facebook which has affected how individuals communicate and spend their free time. In a recent study, Facebook addiction has even been strongly linked to narcissistic behavior and a decline in healthy self-esteem.

Next, let's take a look at some of the most popular psychoanalytic theories of narcissism.

PSYCHOANALYTIC THEORIES ON

NARCISSISM

The understanding and study of narcissism over the years have been strongly influenced by the psychoanalytic theories which have helped in the development of treatment strategies for narcissism and narcissistic personality disorder. The correlation and interconnection between theory, analytic treatment, and conceptualization which are all necessary for theory building which is key to understanding human experiences have over the decades engineered major understanding of the concept which is narcissism.

The psychoanalytic theories which were developed by learned psychoanalysts have helped with the better understanding of, and the procurement of treatment for the narcissistic individual; they have also made it possible and easier to run a diagnosis to portray narcissism in an individual. Through every theoretical development, our understanding of narcissism has evolved. Different authors who have published studies on narcissism have all pinpointed specific core characteristics of narcissism, based on their theoretical point of view.

Theories establish a cause-effect relationship of human phenomenon. There is what we call major theories, there are mini-theories, and there are simple concepts. The psychoanalytic theories on narcissism are all major theories. The first of the popular psychoanalytic theories on narcissism was that of Freud (1910); after that came the studies of Kernberg and Kohut which are recognized as the most popular theories on narcissism in the field of psychoanalytic.

A quick recount of Freud's theory: Freud conceived narcissism as a normal part of human development which stands midway between autoeroticism and object love. During the period of transition, autoerotic sensations which were originally diverse and unconnected fused into the body and became one unified love-object. In his 1914 studies, Freud then aligned his libido theory with narcissism and proclaimed that it developed and transformed into object relationships. Freud proposed that the autoerotic phase is the primary narcissistic condition. This phase became the repository of the libido from which the love of self, and love in general. Freud later recognized narcissism as a developmental process in human, which unfolds over sequential stages. He proposed that obstacles may arise during these sequential stages. He identifies first that a failure might occur which obstructs the smooth transition from self-love to object-love, and second, certain peculiarities may occur in the way an individual expresses narcissistic love. This is one in many of the positions of Freud on libidinal selfcathexis which he also linked to the sequential development of narcissism in humans.

More notable in the field of psychoanalytic are the works of Otto Kernberg and Heinz Kohut which propose an object-relations and self-psychology models respectively to describe the phenomenon known as narcissism and explain the origins of narcissism in humans.

THE THEORY OF KERNBERG ON

NARCISSISTIC PERSONALITY DISORDER

Otto Kernberg's theory on Narcissism is referred to as the "Object Relations theory." According to Kernberg, the concept of a pathological narcissistic individual concentrates around a set of paradoxes: self-exaggeration and an unending need for praise, a charming superficial surface which lays cover to a ruthless interior, and a self-sufficient persona which protects against underlying feelings of malicious envy.

Kernberg believes that the diagnosis of a narcissistic character depends largely on the quality of the individual's object relations and his or her pattern of intrapsychic defenses. What this means is that narcissists experience relationships with others as parasitic and exploitative. They view the world as being between two sets of people-those who have something they can extract and those who do not. They also divide the world between extraordinary people and mediocre ones. To narcissists, extraordinary people are idealized while the other set of people are treated with contempt. However, as much as they idealize this set of extraordinary people, they also fear them; narcissists project their exploitative thoughts and feelings on them and view them as potentially coercive and offensive. Thus, they lack the ability to depend on any object and they fear dependence on another person; a trait which makes their object relations dissatisfying and empty.

Kernberg's theory focuses on how object-relations affect self-esteem. Kernberg described narcissism as a basic part of developing individuals. He referred to it as the libidinal investment of the self. Practically, Kernberg's theory focused on how self-esteem is regulated. He identifies narcissism as having various forms which go thus:

- Normal Adult Narcissism: This is described as the narcissism characteristics in developing individuals. This state of narcissism is achievable due to healthy object relations. What this means is that an individual experiences positive relationships with caretakers at an early age and this results in the internalization of a positive mental concept of the self and objects (people).

- The positive object relations produce an integrated sense of self in the individual. He is able to identify and understand the coexistence of the good and bad in the self and individuals. Also, his superego is able to adapt to the difference between the self and the ideal self. Therefore, a stable concept of self which regulates self-esteem from inside is born.

- Individuals who experience Normal Adult Narcissism possess an inner voice which constantly reminds them that they are good enough. On this basis, they are able to become effective and active in the running of their own lives. They are also able to have a stable moral system while expressing innate human drives such as sexuality and aggression in rational ways.

- Normal Infantile Narcissism: In the early developmental stage of children, their object relations and concept of self are yet to be fully integrated. Thus, children's regulation of self-esteem is partially driven at external gratification. For kids to feel positive about them, they require others to admire them and their possessions such as toys, clothes, dolls and all. However, this is considered appropriate and normal at the early stage of development; it is age appropriate.

- Regression to Normal Infantile Narcissism: This is the pathological form of narcissism in which the superego refuses to mature and stays infantile, thereby retaining childish values and ideals

- Narcissistic Personality Disorder: This is the classic and full-blown pathological form of narcissism. Individuals with narcissistic personality disorder experience aberrations in self-love, the expression of love to others (objects), an irregular moral system and superego. In this sense, self-love points to the traits of self-absorbance. NPD subjects are grandiose and they spend their time fantasizing about excessive love, success, beauty, happiness, and influence. However, this self-love is fueled only by praise and admiration from others and also highly unstable. When narcissistic personality disordered persons experience a view of reality different from their fantasies or perceive an obstacle to the achievement of their grandiose ambitions, it sparks off feelings of depression, extreme anger, and worthlessness.

According to Kernberg, this pathological disorder in individuals develops as a result of pathological object relations in their early developmental stage; the pathological object relations result in a negative internalization of the self and objects. This state births a defense mechanism of splitting, a method where the narcissist characterizes the self and objects as being entirely bad or entirely good. Because of the failure in early relationships with caregivers, the narcissist develops a self-defense mechanism where he creates an unhealthy symbiosis between the self, the ideal self, and the ideal object-a mechanism to become self-sufficient. This means that, in fantasy, the narcissist creates a unification of the desires he has of himself and others, and therefore sheds of the need for dependability on others.

Based on the fact that he takes away the ideal self from the superego and unifies it with the self, the superego becomes weak and excessively strict. Therefore, the narcissist finds it almost impossible to pass the high standards set by the superego. Combines with the absence of comforting object relations to rely on, failure becomes inescapable. If a narcissist is able to pass the overly strict aspiration of the superego, he feels capable and on top of the world, but when they aren't able to reach those aspirations, those feelings crash down with the absence of an internal structure to remind them that they are good enough.

To further explain the Object Relations theory, we can look at it from the perspective of a child who has a distant and un-empathetic mother who is highly critical and devaluing of the child. As a defense mechanism against this lack of love and empathy and protection against emotional pain, the child creates a grandiose internal self. Kernberg posits that the internalization of a grandiose self by the child is usually a combination of 3 distinct elements which are:

- The child's positive traits
- A delusional and fantastical version of himself or herself
- An idealized version of a nurturing parent.

To further keep up with the object-relations model, the child splits off the needy and unlovable image of himself and pushes it to the unconscious where it becomes the basis of a fragile self-esteem, inferior sense of self, and vulnerability as characterized in NPD. Finally,

Kernberg identifies eleven traits of Narcissistic personality disorder which are:

- Excessive absorption with self.
- Superficial effective social adaptation covering the profound disparity in internal relations with others.
- Grandiose delusions and fantasies are coexisting with feelings of inferiority.
- Intense aspirations and ambitions.
- Intense need for admiration and acclaims from others.
- Unhealthy infatuation with power, success, brilliance, beauty, and achievement.
- Inability to love or empathize with others.
- Dissatisfaction with self.
- Exploitation of others.
- Intense and chronic envy.
- Feelings of emptiness and depression.

THE THEORY OF KOHUT ON NARCISSISTIC PERSONALITY DISORDER

Kohut's theory of self-development disagrees largely with the submissions of Freud and Kernberg on narcissism. He rejects the submission of Kernberg that narcissism stems from a defensive withdrawal of object-love relations due to a pattern of parental coldness or vengeful spite.

According to Heinz Kohut and his self-development theory, a narcissistic individual is identified by the transference he or she creates. Kohut's theory is a complete disagreement to the Freudian's view of narcissism which Kernberg built on. While Freud proposed that patients with narcissism were unable to form a transference attachment and as such, cannot be treated with psychoanalytic, Kohut submitted that people with NPD are in fact able to form transference relationships but the transferences are hidden behind traits of aloofness, un-involvement and a habit of treating their therapist as an extension of themselves rather than a separate entity.

Kohut developed the concept of "self-object" to explain the transference phenomena. According to Kohut, the self-object is an individual who performs a necessary role in the maintenance and development of a healthy sense of self. For a child, the parents are the primary self-objects. The parents shape the child's basic struggle for success and power by serving as mirrors through which the child's wish for acknowledgment and exhibitionism reflect. They also serve as objects of the child's idealizing needs; serving as a reinforcement to the child's development of values and goals. A healthy sense of self and the knowledge that feelings and thoughts are a part of one's self are developed based on how the self-objects adequately perform their functions.

In the early narcissism development stage, the child experiences the self-object as part of the self and therefore treats it with the level of control usually reserved for one's mind and body rather than another. With a healthy development of self, the needs of the self-object also mature and become easy to satisfy internally. The child grants the self-object full autonomy and still recognizes the object as part of one's inner life.

However, in a primary disorder such as narcissistic personality disorder, defects, and distortion in the development of the self-manifested in transferential use of others or the therapist as a first self-object. The patient forms either of three pathognomonic transferences which corresponds to the type of self-objects; an idealizing transference, a mirror transference, and a twinship transference.

CHAPTER THREE

NARCISSISTIC ABUSE IN YOUR FAMILY

AND ROMANTIC RELATIONSHIPS

Do you still remember the story of Narcissus which was narrated in an early chapter? Remember how we said the story doesn't end there? Well, the story of Narcissus takes a new turn with the story of Echo, the Woodland Nymph.

Echo was a gorgeous woodland nymph who had been punished by a god who took her voice away and made it possible for her to repeat only what another person says. One day, while Echo was roaming around in the woods, she saw Narcissus and was taken aback by his stunning beauty. Needless to say, Echo was smitten by Narcissus and she falls in love with him. She follows him never leaving his side until he reaches the still silver pond hoping that he would say something nice to her and she would repeat it back to him. When Echo hears Narcissus say "I love you," she was delighted. She imagines that he would love her back when he hears her repeat those same words to him. So, she repeats to Narcissus, "I love you." But to her disappointment, Narcissus was rather too absorbed in his own reflection that he couldn't even hear her, or see her. Devastated, Echo continues to try thinking she would finally get him to see her and tell her he loves her back. Try as she might, her words did not affect her object of affection who was too preoccupied with his own image. Waiting for Narcissus' response, Echo finally withers away and dies waiting for Narcissus to return her love.

You must be thinking, "What a tragic story!" It is a tragic story indeed. However, in truth, the tragic story of Narcissus and Echo is reflective in the relationship between you and the narcissist in your life; it is also reflective in the modern-day relationship with narcissists. Another version of the story says that Narcissus indeed heard Echo but he was disgusted at her love; he was disgusted at the thought that anybody would think they deserve to love him and be loved in return. He was so disgusted that he shouts at Echo and orders her to be silent. This is also typical of a relationship with a narcissist where you invoke his or her wrath by doing something which he disagrees with or doesn't appreciate.

Narcissistic abuse is very much real even though we may not recognize it. Generally, abuse is a fundamental part of any dysfunctional relationship and it comes in different forms. Abuse could be physical, emotional, psychological, verbal, or sexual. However, narcissistic abuse rarely comes in the physical form which makes it difficult to recognize in a relationship. In a relationship with a narcissist, the abuse mostly comes in an emotional, psychological or, verbal form which may make the victim of narcissistic abuse not even know they are being abused. A narcissist will strip you of all self-worth, self-esteem, and value and still have you blame yourself for all the inadequacies in your relationship with them. A narcissist will have you wondering if your life wasn't a worthless one after all and if you couldn't do better to make your relationship work. In the course of the relationship, you will find yourself never blaming the narcissist but yourself. But, you know what's really worse? You'd still want to stay in the relationship, to give it your all and see if everything could work in the end. Like Echo, you will keep on hoping. But, the truth is the abuse never abates because a narcissist can never get rid of his narcissism. That is narcissistic abuse.

To truly understand and recognize narcissistic abuse in your family or romantic relationship, you must first understand narcissism itself. Do you know how they say you have to recognize a problem to even seek a solution to it? Well, that's right. To recover from narcissistic abuse, you must first recognize that it even exists in your relationship. And to recognize narcissistic abuse, you must know what narcissism itself is all about. This is why we began this book by first extensively talking about Narcissism, its forms, its traits, the symptoms and how to understand the intricacies of a narcissist's mind. Knowledge is power:

there is perhaps no truer statement than this. Once you are armed with the basic and required knowledge about narcissism, you will find it easier to handle living with a narcissist or avoid getting in a relationship with another if you have already been in a relationship with one. While the absolute recovery method from narcissistic abuse is accepting the truth about the narcissist in your life and moving on from the relationship, there are some relationships that you can't let go of so easily. There are narcissists everywhere; at work, in the family, among our friends, and our relationship. However, relationships with certain narcissists such as the ones in our family and our love life are not easy to sever so we would rather learn how to cope with them.

Narcissists lack the capacity to truly love themselves, or you for that matter due to their inability to comprehend the nature of feeling. Whatever form of love a narcissist shows at the beginning is superficial and they always end up revealing their true self which they hide behind a facade of charm and self-esteem. Narcissism is driven more by shame than self-esteem. Narcissists have a very fragile self-esteem and an inferior sense of self. A narcissist procures an idealized image of himself which he admires and projects it to others as his true persona. But deep down, he knows that there is a wide gap between the facade he puts up for people and his true shame-driven self which he hides beneath the cloak of superficiality. Therefore, he works extra hard to close up the gap to overcome that feeling of deep shame and inferiority. To do this, he employs certain destructive defense mechanisms which destroy any relationship he has with others and causes pain to his loved ones.

A lot of the coping mechanisms narcissists use is abusive and this was what led to the conception of the term, "narcissistic abuse." This term is not yet recognized or used clinically; it is a layman term. However, narcissistic abuse can be termed as emotional abuse that is committed by a person who is narcissistic or has narcissistic personality disorder. To fight narcissistic abuse, a victim must first identify that there is indeed abuse going on in the relationship. Then, they must build a support system and learn to protect themselves from their abuser.

Narcissistic abuse can manifest in different forms and these are:

- Verbal abuse: This includes bullying, belittling, blaming, accusing, shaming, demeaning, devaluing, criticizing, threatening, undermining, opposing and name-calling. Most people occasionally blame, criticize, block, or oppose others but this doesn't make it narcissistic abuse. To term it narcissistic abuse, you must consider the frequency at which the verbal assaults occur, the malice and the context in which they occur.

- Manipulation: This is a form of passive aggression, and is an indirect way of influencing someone to behave in a way that benefits the manipulator and furthers his goals. Usually, manipulation seems cool and maybe even harmless on the surface but beneath it all, you feel a sense of hostility and demeaning. You may not even recognize when you're being manipulated.

- Gaslighting: This is a form of narcissistic abuse in which the narcissists distorts your view of reality. He convinces you to distrust your view of reality and gets you to believe that you are mentally incapable. Think of a partner who constantly does something wrong and makes you believe it is all your fault such that you don't even recognize when he is the one doing something wrong anymore.

- Emotional blackmail: Abuse can also come in the form of emotional blackmail. This may include threats, intimidation, warnings, anger, and punishment. Emotional blackmail results in doubt of yourself. It results in feelings of fare, guilt or obligation.

- Negative contrasting: The narcissist intentionally makes negative comparisons of you with himself/herself or other people.

- Exploitation: The narcissist takes advantage of you for his personal ends without consideration of your feelings or thoughts.

- Neglect: This form of narcissistic abuse is mostly common in the mother-child relationship. The narcissistic mother or caregiver neglects the needs of the child who is supposed to be their responsibility

- Withholding: The narcissist withholds affection, love, sex, money and other things from you.

- Invasion of privacy: The abuser disregards boundaries by checking through your personal things such as mail, phone, or texts. He also denies you your physical privacy by consistently stalking you and invading your personal life.

- Deception: Unending lies and deceptions to avoid taking responsibility for their actions.

- Sabotage: Disruptively interfering with your relationships or endeavors for revenge or personal gains.

- Financial abuse: This includes controlling you through economic domination or extorting, stealing, manipulating, or gambling to drain you of your personal finances.

- Isolation: Restricting your interactions with family, friends in a bid to isolate you, manipulate, control, and abuse you without hindrance.
- Violence: Pulling your hair, blocking your movement, throwing things and destroying your things.

The condition suffered by victims of narcissistic abuse has been given a name and is called "Echoism," coined from the name of Echo the Woodland nymph who fell in love with Narcissus and suffered the consequence of unrequited love. The concept of Echoism has been made popular by Dr. Craig Malkin, a psychologist who published a book titled "Rethinking Narcissism" where he expounds on the concept of echoism which was coined first by psychoanalyst Dean Davis.

Echoism is typically a term used to describe being in a toxic relationship with a narcissist. The narcissist may be the parent, partner, friend or sibling of the echoist. Usually, echoists are compassionate, highly-sensitive, empathic and emotionally intelligent people who also double as a people pleaser. Compassionate and highly empathic people who have been or are being exploited by narcissists in a relationship are likely to become echoists. According to Dr. Malkin, echoists have a fear of being selfish, needy or special; therefore it is easy for the narcissist to take advantage of them.

Narcissistic abuse can transform an empathic person from a person who is in touch with their own self to an echo of the narcissist in their life. Narcissistic abuse causes the victims to become invisible, lose touch with their sense of self and practically become the shadow of their abuser. Often, adults who have experienced narcissistic abuse right from childhood unconsciously seek out partners with narcissistic tendencies.

SIGNS YOU WERE RAISED BY A

NARCISSISTIC PARENT

Have you ever been in a conversation where you practically just sat there and felt like you were there to watch the other person's reality show and you simply just watch? Or maybe they are sharing their problems with you and they exaggerate them so much to make you believe your own problems were smaller in comparison to theirs? A persistent pattern of this kind of trait is referred to as Narcissistic personality disorder and you may have experienced it with either of your parents while growing up.

Many therapists believe cutting narcissistic people out of your life is the best solution to narcissistic abuse. However, what if this abuser is actually your parent; the very people who birthed and raised you? Growing up with a narcissistic parent can take its toll on you and place a strain in your relationship. However, you might not even consider your parent as being narcissistic or subjecting you to any form of abuse.

When you're raised in a narcissistic household or by a narcissistic parent, you tend to hold them to a higher standard than everybody else. You are unable to see anything wrong with whatever they do, and even though there might be some feelings in your guts telling you the way you are being treated by your parent is wrong; you learn to accept their narcissistic abuse as the norm. Thankfully, there are signs to check out if you want to know whether either of your parents is narcissistic.

- They set unrealistically high standards for you: Parents with NPD often set very high standards for themselves and this extends to their kids. They see you as an extension of themselves and as such, they force you to achieve some unrealistically high standards which they have set for you. A narcissistic parent will always see her child as being exceptional, very good looking extraordinary and special from the others-beyond reasonable doubt. This sort of attitude can affect others such as the child's teacher, classmates or tutor. For instance, a narcissistic parent may frequently contact their child's school to ensure he is ahead in his class and doing better than others.

- They have no interest in your life: Have you ever felt like your parent never bothered with what's happening in your life while you were growing up? Instead, they constantly bombard you with details of everything going on in their own life? If your parent is the type that tells you to put on a happy face even when you're feeling otherwise, this is a sign that they are narcissistic. Due to the lack of empathy which is a fundamental trait in narcissism, your parent finds it difficult to connect with you emotionally and so; they lack interest in you or your activities. If you are the type who grew up sweeping your feelings under the carpet without letting them out to your parent or anybody else, it may be a sign that you suffered narcissistic abuse from your parent. Often, the narcissistic mother or father is too preoccupied with their own needs, feelings and thoughts to tend to that of the child. Ideally, parents are meant to put their children's needs first but with someone who lacks the ability to empathize, that is a quite impossible feat to achieve.

- They make you feel like you're the parent: If you grew up performing the duties of a caregiver rather than being the child that you are, it is another sign that your parent exploited you while growing up. A narcissistic parent exploits the child in ways such as borrowing money from the child without repaying. Or, maybe the parent praises compliments or does something nice for the child while expecting the child to return the gesture in larger folds.

- They expect you to worship them: A domineering or narcissistic parent often wants a lot of attention and admiration from their child. For instance, they may expect you to follow an order or instruction without as much as a question or disagreement. If you don't give them the attention and admiration they need, they become angry and lash out at you without remorse.

- They believe you are perfect: Every parent might wish for their child to be perfect but for narcissists, they take this belief to an extreme. This is usually caused by the narcissistic parent projecting their narcissism on their child by regarding them as perfect and special. A typical narcissistic parent will regard any negative feedback about the child as envy or jealousy, and others being 'out to get' the child.

The problem with narcissistic parents lies in the fact that they try to live through their children. To achieve this, they immerse themselves in every of the child's interests, activities an accomplishments. But most times, they take more than they give. Even though they do it subconsciously, a narcissistic parent feeds his/her own superego through the achievement of the child. The problem with the parent's investment in the life of their child is that it is hardly selfless or out of parental love. Rather, it is a way they can project the accomplishments of the child as theirs.

Another problem is that while it seems like they are being supportive like an ideal parent; narcissistic parents usually grow competitive with their child. They want the child's success and achievements to reflect on them and garner attention and praises towards them, but they become angry and vengeful when it seems like they are being overshadowed by the child's achievements. This way, they prevent the child from developing a healthy sense of self-esteem. Rather, they use the child as a means of drawing attention to themselves. The only use a narcissistic parent has for their children is to use them to reflect favorably on them, thereby using the children in a way that is hurtful and disregarding. Narcissistic parents have a terribly low supply of healthy self-esteem and they try to compensate for this through their children.

If you have been raised by a narcissistic parent, you may find yourself exhibiting some of these traits:

- You blame yourself: Instead of blaming your parent for the way they treat you, you develop the habit of blaming yourself for all of their inadequacies instead. Narcissistic abuse causes the child victim to sacrifice his self-esteem and take responsibility for all the negativity and nastiness he experiences. You start to believe that it is your fault that your narcissistic parent doesn't love you. You also believe that if you try harder and change yourself, you can get your parent to love you as much as you want them to. But the truth is they never will; narcissists lack the capacity for experiencing true love or expressing feelings.

- You feel and act invisible: Due to the emotional and psychological abuse by your narcissistic father or mother, you lost touch with your sense of self. Child victims of narcissistic abuse usually have no sense of self or an idea of what they need or want. The parent's grandiose self eclipses the child totally and begets a person who does not know who they are as an individual. You become unable to identify your own feelings, needs or thoughts not just to your abuser but also to other people around you; that feeling of invisibility and not making yourself count.

- Acclimation to Narcissism or Aversion to Relationships: Being raised by a narcissistic parent will result in either of two things in the child's relationships; becoming so acclimated to narcissism that he unconsciously seeks out narcissistic relationships or becomes averted to relationship as a whole. The lack of empathy, the abuse, rage, and neglect from the parent becomes overwhelming to the point where the child naturally expects the exact kind of treatment in every relationship. They may also develop insecure attachments or breed a distrust for people and an aversion to emotional commitment altogether. This makes the child unable to commit to emotions.

- Co-dependency, guilt and a cycle of Narcissism: Children who have been abused by narcissistic parents often adapt by erasing their individualism, sacrificing their needs or becoming narcissists themselves. It's a cycle! Children who are raised by narcissistic parents have very high tendencies of becoming narcissists themselves or losing themselves and becoming narcissists' pleaser.

Why do Narcissistic Parents Overly Connect to their Children?

The reasons for this vary. However, the major reason why narcissistic parents immerse themselves deeply into a child's life is so the kid's performance can reflect on them. The reasons for this are quite complicated. Sometimes, the narcissistic parent may be trying to make up for what they regard as their own shortcomings. They may also depend on their child's accomplishment to bolster up their own sense of self. By doing this, they fail to see the child as an autonomous and unique individual capable of having his own feelings, thoughts, and emotions. They see the child as an extension of themselves and fail to realize that he or she is a separate entity who is capable of making his own decisions and experiencing feelings or emotions. This is caused by emotional hunger on the part of the parent which causes them to feed off the child's own achievements.

SIGNS YOU ARE IN A RELATIONSHIP WITH A NARCISSISTIC PARTNER

A relationship with a narcissist can be a toxic one. However, narcissists are almost always unidentifiable in that cloak of superficial charms and love they drape. Many people are in a relationship with a narcissist, and they don't even realize it. You may be married to a narcissist, and you won't know it; this is because you are oblivious of the very obvious traits exhibited by narcissistic partners. Often, people also mistake chronic insecurity from a partner as traits of narcissism. However, if you are in a relationship where you constantly get into an endless roll of high-drama arguments with your partner over the same issue; that's a very red flag telling your partner is a narcissist.

In the early stage of a relationship, most people often have that deep feeling in their guts alerting them that there's something terribly wrong in this relationship, but like all new people in love, they often ignore their guts. Usually, that feeling in your gut is just your inner voice saying this relationship isn't normal, look at all the nasty behaviors your partner makes you put up with.

It is important that you learn to spot the traits of narcissism and narcissistic abuse in your relationship before it takes a hold of you. So, how do you know if your partner is narcissistic or if they are abusing you? There are different telltale signs to watch out for.

1. Your partner shrinks your world.

Narcissists are jealous and possessive by nature. They want to control your life and dictate the events in it. Perhaps you are the type who likes to visit your parents or siblings. Maybe you just enjoy chatting with them on the phone instead. You might also be the type of person who likes to hang out with friends or go to the gym. Well, you narcissistic partner simply won't take that from you. They will accuse you of ignoring them or your kids. A narcissist will tell you that you are putting others before your relationship with them and convince you that you have your priorities wrong. To avoid arguments, you will probably start to turn down invitations automatically. You may also sign out of that gym membership, and find a way to let yourself off the next time your friends say you should chill at the beach. You also start getting secretive with the way you call or visit your family. In a bid to make them happy and show that you are actually committed to the relationship, you start to do less of those things that make you happy. On days when you decide to pay a quick visit to a friend anyway, your narcissistic partner takes it as proof of your disregard for the relationship. So you have it; they are shrinking your world little by little and building it around just the relationship.

This might have seemed a little cute if your partner wants it because they can't get enough of you and they actually want more. However, don't expect your partner to start showering you with all of their attention and care just because you make them your priority; they will simply ignore you and stay preoccupied with themself. Now, if you try to complain to your partner about the lack of attention from them after you canceled a plan just because they wanted you to, it will bring you to the second sign that you are indeed in a relationship with a narcissist.

2. Your partner never accepts the blame.

Typical narcissism: it is always someone else's fault and that someone is almost always you. It is quite simple: do something they dislike, it is your fault; they do something you dislike, it is still your fault. A narcissist always has tons of excuses available for their bad behaviors, but yours are largely inexcusable. If your partner is narcissistic, they most likely never admit that their hurtful and manipulative behavior is not appropriate. Instead, they will accuse you of being oversensitive and reactive. But in truth, your narcissistic partner is the one who does exactly that; take everything personally, no matter how small.

3. Your partner projects all of their unfavorable qualities onto you.

You know all those bad attitudes you are sure your partner exhibits in your relationship? No, that's not them, it's you. Well, that's what they think. They are not manipulative, you are. They aren't controlling, but you are. Selfishness? No, that's still you. A narcissistic partner will accuse you of all the bad behaviors on earth when in fact; they are the ones who exhibit these behaviors. Your partner will accuse you of keeping them in the dark when they are in truth the one who is always secretive about many things. Now, the thing is in a relationship like that where you're being emotionally abused; you will out of fear of argument go behind your partner to do a lot of stuff like spending money, paying a friend a visit and so on. When your narcissistic partner finds out what you have been doing behind their back, they take it as proof of the lack of trust they have in you and use this as a way of exerting even more control on you. The thing is, you just can't win with a narcissist.

4. Your partner exhibits double-standard.

It is quite difficult to win an argument with a narcissistic individual; they simply will never admit that they are wrong. Narcissists have a strong sense of entitlement which makes them believe they are an exception to the rules. However, for them to exert control over you, then the rules must count. If you accuse a narcissist of double-standard, they will find a way to make you look dumb or give you an excuse from their never-ending well of excuses. If you catch your narcissistic partner red-handed doing something they would never allow you to do, they will still put the blame on you contemptuously.

They do this in different ways. For instance, they may admit that they did something wrong, but they'll shift the focus to you by accusing you of doing it all the time too. They may get enraged and say you don't have the right to accuse them of anything, considering "all they put up with in the relationship." They may say you are unforgiving and intolerant. If you reference the incident in a later circumstance, they will accuse of you bearing grudges. To muddle it all up the more, you'll be surprised that the rules change at their will. Therefore, they accuse you whenever it suits their narrative and is to their advantage. Thus, you begin to lose touch with the sense of right or wrong. That's how much they can manipulate you. What next? You start to feel crazy.

5. You feel mentally incomplete.

The aim of your narcissistic partner is to throw you off-balance. A narcissist wants you to doubt yourself, not them. Once they achieve this, you start to question your feelings and perceptions resulting in a feeling of mental incompetence. This is the major reason why victims of narcissistic abuse remain in the relationship. The narcissist has influenced their sense of perception into thinking there are some major flaws with them which others may not want and so, they stick with the abuser because they believe he is right to find flaws with them.

Keep it in mind that narcissists rarely seek out other narcissists like them. Rather, they find people like you who are willing to identify their own flaws rather than blame others; people who try to be fair and extra-cooperative in their relationship; people who are willing to take less than they give. These are the kind of people that are easy to manipulate for the narcissist. Once such a relationship results in kids or having property together, it becomes even more challenging for the victim of narcissistic abuse to leave the relationship. This builds up to another point on signs exhibited by a narcissistic partner.

6. Your partner doesn't handle rejection well.

If you reject a narcissist, they will seek you out and have their revenge. Psychology refers to this as "narcissistic injury": a situation where a narcissist feels challenged, hurt, wronged or made to look dumb. For a person with a grandiose sense of self, that is intolerable, and they will never forgive you until they have had their pound of flesh. This can take the form of angry texts in mild cases, and financial punishment in extreme cases.

DEFUSING A BOMB: UNDERSTANDING AND LIVING WITH THE NARCISSIST

Have you ever watched one of those movies where there's a military man or whoever trying to defuse a bomb? Do you notice there's always a pattern that is followed in these movies?

The military man comes, and he knows there is a bomb; but he has to be careful with the bomb. So, he doesn't just rush ahead like a hero trying to defuse the bomb; that will get him and a whole lot of other people killed. No, he has to be really delicate through the whole defusing process. Now, the whole process of defusing a bomb cuts across six stages.

- Knowing when to defuse the bomb: Understand if this is a person worth "defusing."
- Know where the bomb has been planted: Understand where the abuse is coming from.
- Enter the bomb site and get rid of all enemies: In this case, your enemy is the facade the narcissist is putting on.
- Locate the bomb: Find the core of the narcissism. How bad is the level of narcissism?

- Start defusing very delicately: Once you know how bad, you can tell the best way to approach this; which is always the delicate way.

Understanding a narcissist and living with one can be compared to this same process of defusing a bomb. Like bombs, narcissists have the tendency to explode all up in your face if you do not tread cautiously.

To live with a narcissist, you must first recognize that the person is indeed a narcissist. Don't make the mistake of confusing narcissism for another personality or mental health disorder. Once you know for sure that "yeah, this is a narcissist!" you can go ahead and follow the tips on living with a narcissistic parent and a narcissistic partner!

TIPS FOR COPING WITH A NARCISSISTIC PARENT

Living and coping with a narcissistic parent is quite challenging, but it's achievable if you follow the tips below.

- Recognize the abnormality in their behavior: People generally like to solve or work out a problem in a way that is mutually agreeable by all parties involved. However, a narcissistic person enjoys the power play. For narcissistic parents or parents with suspicious NPD traits, you either take their way or the highway. Rather than create excuses for their behaviors and looking for a way to make it about you or something you did wrong, recognize and accept that there is something terribly wrong with their actions. If your parent values the ability to control you over a functional relationship between you both, you should recognize that this sort of behavior isn't a healthy or normal one. Recognize them for who they are, and it becomes easier to cope with them.

- Set boundaries: Narcissists have no respect for boundaries. They don't even know what a boundary is. Typical of a narcissist, a narcissistic parent will always overstep boundaries just to prove to you that they can. They may make a habit of it by inviting themselves to events, give presents to 'special' family members only or disregard their partner's wish on how they want to interact with the children. To prevent them from imposing their will on you, you must also make it a habit to enforce consequences for their bad behaviors. Doing this might make you feel like you are disciplining a 5-year-old, but that's ultimately the way to treat a person who acts selfishly like a child anyway.

- Resist any attempt of gaslighting: To further control you, a narcissistic parent will find ways by which they can delude you into believing your perception of right and wrong is wrong. This is a manipulation tactic narcissists employ to distort your view of reality and yourself. For instance, a narcissistic parent might recount stories of your negative behaviors which never occurred just to get you to believe that they actually happened. They may also convince you into believing you remember certain events incorrectly. Although you may not be able to remember everything with perfect accuracy, it is important that you resist every of their attempt to dictate to you or influence your perception of reality.

- Accept that people won't understand your situation: This is the gospel truth. People who have no prior experience or knowledge of NPD will find it difficult to understand you even if you tell them what you are being put through. They will give you the most unhelpful advice and remind you "your mom is the one mother you will ever have. You have got to sort things out." Unless your parent seeks therapy or treatment for their disorder, they will never change. Thus, you must accept this rather than trying to get people who won't understand the whole situation.

- Realize that cutting ties may be the way to go: As much as you may try to make them work, some things won't just work out and one of such things is your relationship with your narcissistic parent who is unwilling to accept that there is a problem. If you cut off or criticize a narcissistic parent and then try to make things work, they will only see that as an opportunity to get you to pay for the 'wrong' you did. When it gets to a stage where you need to sever ties, it becomes apparent. Cutting ties off with your parent is a really hard and painful thing to do, but it is necessary for your own mental health.

If you have to cope with narcissistic parents, you have to realize that there are tons of people like you out there also trying and you aren't alone. You can consult helpful articles, join support groups online and share your story with people who have experienced similar situations. Doing this will make the whole process easier on you.

TIPS FOR LIVING WITH A NARCISSISTIC PARTNER

Not all narcissistic partners are meant to be cast away like old cloth. Sometimes, we have just got to realize how to handle them and make it all work. However, once you recognize that the relationship doesn't look like it could work, you must take the fastest horse and gallop off to a better life.

Often, people who are with a narcissistic partner think "I know he/she is a narcissist, but I don't want to leave. How do I make it all work?" When they ask this type of question, they already know the standard response would be "Leave" or "Let it go." However, they have made up their mind to make the relationship a functioning one. This may be because they are in love, or they have children together. Their religious belief may also be a major better in determining whether they stay with their narcissistic partner and try to make the relationship a successful one. To survive living with a narcissist, you must be prepared to:

- Understand what being a narcissist really means
- What is practically possible and what is not.
- What your boundaries are

You already know what it means to be a narcissist based on all the different traits of the narcissist which we have discussed. Therefore, let's move on to identifying those things that are realistically possible or not.

- Accept that the narcissist in your life will never take responsibility and you are okay with that. Narcissists always see just two choices before them; be perfect or be worthless. Therefore, they find it hard to take the blame or accept responsibility for anything they do wrong. They regard accepting blame as an admittance that they are worthless and heavily flawed; therefore they will never do it. This, you must be willing to recognize and accept. Most times, you will have to be the one to take the blame for all the faults in the relationship. Decide whether you're willing to put up with that for the rest of your life.

- Accept that you will never get an apology for whatever wrong they commit. Due to their inability to take responsibility for their actions, narcissists find it even harder to apologize. Even when he clearly knows he was wrong, your narcissistic partner will not apologize, and you must accept that for reality. Often, a narcissistic partner who knows they did something wrong may make a reparative gesture by getting a gift to make up for what they did. You must be able to accept their reparative gesture and let go of the need for an apology if you really want to make the relationship work.

- In your relationship with a narcissist, the best thing is to always pick your battles. You can't demand an apology for every little insult, or you will find yourself arguing over the same thing all through the week. You should be prepared to disregard minor, unintended insults. You must carefully pick your battles. If you complain to your narcissistic partner every single time he or she does something to wrong you, your relationship will turn sour, you will always be in one conflict or another, and there really won't be anything to be happy about. Save your fighting energy for the major battles like when they do something serious and intentional and cross certain boundaries which they shouldn't have. If you let them get away with it all the time, narcissists will do and say anything they feel like.

- After a fight with your narcissistic partner, you may find that they are unwilling to process the fight and discuss what went wrong. To them, this may seem like a way of rubbing their nose in their mistakes. To do this, consider using the "we" language so as not to make it feel like you are pinning all the blame on them. Also, avoid sounding accusatory. For instance: "I know we both love each other and we're willing to put in our all to make this relationship work. I wish we both could be a little more careful the things that set us off."

- Decide what your boundaries are, and defend them with all your might. What this means is that you have to make it clear to your narcissistic partner what is tolerable and what is intolerable of their bad behaviors to you. If you leave them to it, a narcissist will step on all reasonable boundaries because they don't even know there are boundaries anyway, which is why you have to define them for him or her. If you do not draw certain boundaries around something such as verbal abuse, it may escalate into physical abuse. Therefore, you must make your boundaries clear right from the start.

To live with a narcissistic partner is a difficult but achievable feat. It may not be easy, but it will run more smoothly if you have already taken the time to educate yourself on what to realistically expect from a narcissist, and learn a few tips on how you can deal with and handle bad narcissistic behavior in your boyfriend or spouse. Finally, define your boundaries clearly and defend them even if it means leaving the narcissist and moving on.

CHAPTER FOUR

THERE'S A ROAD CALLED RECOVERY FROM NARCISSISTIC ABUSE

Narcissistic abuse is a maliciously intent force that draws you in, suck you dry, tosses you out and leave you with battered self-esteem, post-traumatic stress, a stark sense of worthlessness and self-contempt. That is how bad narcissistic abuse can be.

Narcissistic abuse hijacks your identity and leaves you with a skewed version of yourself whom you don't even understand. The traumas and horror that come with narcissistic personality disorder feel like they will never leave you. As a person who has been narcissistically abused, you are even more prone to further abuse and manipulation. You carry a whole lot of emotional and psychological baggage with you, and sometimes you even feel like a victim. To worsen the whole situation, you are perpetually in a state of anxiety and confusion that leaves you unable to reclaim your identity and your life back. You have no idea how to start on the path to recovery or if there's even a path to recovery at all.

This is true: narcissistic abuse can leave you feeling like you have no willpower or the power required to fight back and take action. However, all you need is a little bit of support and intervention to get the zeal to make a difference and take control of your life back. To recover from narcissistic abuse by your parent or your partner, you must first ensure that you recognize the symptoms of narcissistic abuse; usually, people who are being abused may not even recognize it. It is after this that you will truly be able to fight back and get the pieces of your life back together. Once you light the spark, there's no telling how brightly your fire will burn. But first, light the spark.

SURVIVING NARCISSISTIC ABUSE FROM YOUR PARENT

The journey of recovery from narcissistic abuse which started right from childhood is probably the toughest. To recover from this type of emotional abuse, you must repair your damaged reality- that distorted view of reality that was enabled by the kind of damaging parenting you experienced. Narcissistic abuse is a serious interpersonal trauma; therefore recovering from it isn't a situation where you try to work on the relationship with your mother. There is simply no working on anything here.

When you are raised by a narcissistic parent, you're conditioned to believe that only the voice of that parent matters. You will believe that only that person has the right to have and express feelings or opinions. Unconsciously, you will stave off your needs to satisfy those of your parent. Due to all this childhood conditioning, it becomes difficult to adopt a healthier lifestyle as an adult. However, with these tips you will be learning below, you can heal from the childhood abuse you were put through. While seeing a therapist might be the best way to go, these tips will also help complement all your therapeutic sessions.

- Build Self-Compassion: This may prove challenging for you. Trying to develop self-compassion triggers flashbacks to all those years where you were abused, and compassion was usually a key part of the next attack. It is also difficult since you grew up with an emotionally neglectful parent, and you have no idea how it feels like to receive compassion. Compassion is absent in a narcissist, thanks to their lack of empathy. Thus, how do you learn compassion if the one person that was meant to teach you that from childhood doesn't even know what it is? Quite hard, you will agree. However, you have to be patient with the whole process. Think about the nice things others have said to you in the past or the other nice things you'd say to others if they were in a situation like yours: say these things to yourself regularly. Create kindheartedness towards yourself, and stop pushing yourself so hard.

- Get rid of that inner critic: There's an inner child somewhere in you still hoping that if it becomes smarter, more helpful and flawless, your parent will start to show it the love it wants. The inability to achieve this after consistent tries result in the child concluding that it is unlovable and defective, and this leads to a process of self-criticism. To get rid of this inner critic, you must be willing to become open around safe people. As you meet more people like this, sharing your story with them will help you ease up on the criticism you dole out to yourself non-stop and eventually, you'll be able to get rid of the toxic shame you feel inside.

- Develop self-trust: Create a visual image of that inner child in you and start building a comforting, secure and strong relationship with it. The ideal way to build self-trust is to begin to treat yourself well and better than you used to. Stop rejecting your true self and start repairing the damage caused by your parent. Get rid of that skewed person they built and embrace your real self with warmth.

- Exercise self-care: All those years with your narcissistic parent has trained you to concentrate on their reactions only, ignoring your own feelings. You have been conditioned to focus externally and thus, have no idea how to recognize your own needs. Start on a journey of self-care to repair this conditioning. Conceive an "inner nurturer" and let its presence be strong and dominant in your life. Pen down a list of all the happy things you can do for yourself every passing day.

Recovery from narcissistic abuse, especially when it starts from childhood is a process, and it may take a long while, but you will get there eventually. You must allow yourself the lenience of time, grace, and unhurried baby steps. Be mindful of what you are experiencing. Try as much as possible to avoid getting into another narcissistic relationship. Eliminate the critic inside of your head, and more importantly, learn to develop a healthy relationship with self and others.

RECOVERING FROM NARCISSISTIC ABUSE

IN A ROMANTIC RELATIONSHIP

Here are tips to follow to recover from narcissistic abuse from your romantic relationship;

Identify the symptoms of narcissistic abuse in your relationship. It is manipulative, intrusive, one-sided, rid, oppressive, and exhausting. Knowing these symptoms will help you remember that your relationship is abnormal.

- Stop acting like the victim. The more you view yourself as a victim, the more you encourage narcissism. Our experiences in life may be built to shape us. However, it is up to us to let them define us. Rather than considering yourself a victim of narcissism, change the perception to you being a target. For reasons unknown to you, you ended up with a narcissist of all persons. This can happen to anybody, not just you. The moment you become aware of the destructive effects of narcissism and how damaging it has been to your life, you gain the power of choice. Would you rather be a powerless victim or a target who resists manipulation? Overwrite your past experiences and work towards creating new ones.

- Build up a narcissism-proof space for yourself. The road to recovery from narcissistic abuse is a very long and torturous one. This is because narcissists take away the greatest asset you have: your space. Every human needs a physical space to feel safe, a psychological space to think and reason, and emotional space to connect with our inner self. But, narcissists strip you of all spaces you have so you can become isolated within yourself. To recover from this, you must learn to build up new spaces for yourself; somewhere they can't reach you. Example of these safe spaces may be solitude, the therapist's office, meditation and so on.

- Recognize the challenges ahead of you as you try to recover. It is very important that you identify all the obstacles that may face your way as you work towards rediscovering yourself. Obstacles are created in our minds. Once we refuse to pay them mind, they lose the power they have over us. Examples of obstacles you may come across as you try to heal from narcissistic abuse are; love starvation, mind control, and guilt.

- Look beyond the abuse. Often, targets of narcissistic abuse lose their heart because they have forgotten how to use and what it feels like to have a heart. Recovering from narcissistic abuse is all about regaining your mind, and reclaiming your true self. You must never forget that.

CHAPTER FIVE

TREATMENT FOR PEOPLE WITH

NARCISSISTIC PERSONALITY DISORDER

Mental health disorders are usually treated with a combination of medication and therapy. However, medication doesn't work for personality disorders such as Narcissistic Personality Disorder. The only thing that works for treating narcissistic personality disorder is therapy.

For people with NPD, a therapy program that offers individual, family and group therapy is usually the best option for recovery and treatment. Intensive long-term therapy can help a narcissist come to term with how damaging their condition has been to their life, and how it has stalled them from reaching their full potential. Getting family, friends and loved ones to share their input can also add depth to these realizations. Since narcissism is an organizing principle of personality for people with NPD, therapists avoid attacking the condition aggressively. Therapists tackle the process deliberately and cautiously to avoid pushing the patient too far too fast.

In therapy, the therapist and narcissistic patient work hard together to identify the behaviors and attitudes that create conflict, dissatisfaction and also serve as stressors in the patient's life. As the therapeutic process continues, the therapist encourages the patient to take constructive and decisive actions that will help neutralize the negative impacts of their narcissistic behavior, giving them practical tips and instructions that will help them. The therapist avoids creating a judgmental environment and focuses strictly on finding solutions for the patient. This is very important as only a positive approach to therapy will help build trust and confidence between the doctor and the patient. It will enable them to communicate more effectively.

Therapy programs which have been proven to help patients diagnosed with Narcissistic Personality Disorder include:

- Cognitive Behavioral Therapy: Through multiple CBT sessions, NPD patients can learn to replace distorted and delusional thoughts with more realistic and positive ideas and self-assessments.

- Psychodynamic therapy: In psychodynamic therapeutic sessions, the therapist encourages the patient to delve into the depth of their past experiences. This will allow them to assess the effects of turbulent relationships on their lives, and also to examine unconscious assumptions they have about themselves and others who enable their narcissistic attitudes.

- Family therapy: Narcissistic attitudes affect the family as much as they affect the patient. Therefore, involving the loved ones in the recovery and healing process can help the NPD patient realize just how much their self-centeredness affect their loved ones in all ramifications.

Narcissistic individuals are often resistant to any form of therapy, especially in the early stages. Therefore, the mental health therapist must ensure that the NPD patient is compliant with every of their treatment plan and process. As a narcissist, cooperation won't come naturally for you. But to truly recover, you must learn to work together with your therapy for the solution to your problem.

PRACTICAL TIPS FOR WORKING ON YOUR NARCISSISM OR NARCISSISTIC PERSONALITY DISORDER

You didn't choose to be a narcissist, but here you are a narcissist. The causes of pathological narcissism are complex and deep-rooted. Most narcissists aren't even aware of their destructive and negative behavioral patterns, and this result in them having to learn about life the hard way. As a narcissist, your chronic negative attitudes can result in some consequences which include isolation, estrangement, divorce, loneliness, cut-offs from friends and family and damaged reputation.

Thankfully, as a self-aware narcissist who is currently reading this book, there are steps you can take towards reforming yourself and making a change in the destructive pattern.

- Become aware of boundaries

To sustain a mutual relationship with anybody, you have to become cognizant of where the self ends and where another individual begins. Stop seeing humans as an extension of yourself and start seeing them as separate individuals. When you become aware of boundaries, you can work on not violating or overstepping them. Recognizing boundaries will help reduce personal and work relationship fallouts, and help improve and normalize your relationship with others.

- Practice Mindfulness

The art of mindfulness means thinking before you act. Becoming mindful allows you to become more considerate and thoughtful in your actions. It means putting yourself in the shoes of others. If a person comes late for a date with you, consider the fact that they may have encountered a few difficulties and not just jump into conclusion that they did it to annoy you. When talking to others or giving an opinion, consider how it might sound to the person you're talking to. Being mindful means considering the way you might feel if someone else talked to you the exact way you talk to them. Learn to treat others the way you'd like them to treat you.

- Develop Substance

For a narcissist trying to recover, developing substance is essential. What this means is that you should try to shed off that fake skin you put on for people and seek out the real you. Doing this will result in some benefits which include; reducing stress, anxiety and moral conflict. It will also increase the durability of your personal and professional relationships.

- Seek Help and Support

You can't walk through the recovery road alone; you'll need a companion. Being a person with NPD can be a lonesome experience especially since you believe you have few equals in the world. This will make it difficult for you to discuss your struggles and insecurities with the people in your life. As you become more aware and cognizant of your flaws, consider reaching out to a trained and qualified therapist for guidance in working through your issues. Also, try to register in appropriate support groups which are facilitated by licensed and experienced mental health professionals. Taking a step as brave as this requires honesty and courage on your part and you may encounter a lot of ups and downs. However, it can be gratifying once you start to notice the impacts. You are on a journey to self-rediscovery, and you simply shouldn't go through it alone! Seeking help increases your sense of awareness, belongingness, facilitates the healing process and finally, it ameliorates your struggles in isolation.

- Don't be hard on yourself

As a narcissist who has become self-aware, you may experience feelings of regrets, shame, and remorse at the damages you have done to yourself and others. You may see yourself as an evil person and feel overwhelmed with guilt. These are normal. However, during this process, you must also remember to be gentle with yourself. Remember that it isn't your fault and you have also gone through a lot; don't forget that you were denied your humanity at an early age. Now that you are self-aware work towards creating healthier relationships with yourself and people in your life rather than staying stuck in the past. Discuss your experience with your therapist in-depth to aid faster growth and healing.

GENERAL IMPROVEMENT TIPS FOR

NARCISSISTIC PEOPLE

- Address people by their names when speaking or writing.
- Listen to others as much as you talk.
- Be genuinely curious and interested about people in your life.
- Ask questions and give opinions carefully.
- Keep your promises, agreements, and appointments.
- Avoid making promises you know you can't or won't keep
- Be accountable and stop blaming others for your actions. Take responsibility when necessary.
- Avoid taking actions or making decisions that neglect the feelings of the people around you.
- Think things through carefully before blurting them out.
- Be mindful of your words and actions.
- Stop making everything be all about you!

CONCLUSION

Congratulations! You have successfully made it to the end of Narcissistic Abuse: Understanding Narcissistic Personality Disorder and Healing from Narcissistic Abuse. Well, that was a long read, but it was entertaining and educating all through, wouldn't you agree? You have learned quite a lot about narcissism in one book.

Through the course of reading this book, you must have gained detailed knowledge on the subject of Narcissism and its components. You should now be able to talk about narcissism more broadly without a touch of layman's understanding.

This book is aimed at helping individuals better understand narcissism. It focuses on helping targets of Narcissistic Abuse recognize the abuse, why they are being abused and ultimately, start on a journey towards rediscovering themselves!

ABOUT THE AUTHOR

Charlotte Reed is a restorative coach, author, primary school teacher and has been working with children for over five years. Charlotte lives with her husband and their daughter. When Charlotte isn't working, you can find her reading poems or listening to music. Her interests include psychology, sociology, education, self-care, comprehensive human development. Charlotte has a weakness for chocolate and flowers.

In her coaching practice, she works with people who have one or more narcissist in their lives (parents, spouse). Her new book, Defusing the Bomb: A Guide To Understanding And Dealing with a Narcissist and Healing From Narcissistic Abuse explains what narcissism really means, how to recognize narcissism and deal with narcissistic abuse.